MASHED POTATOES

Collecting Data

Nancy Harris

Rourke
Publishing LLC
Vero Beach, Florida 32964

© 2008 Rourke Publishing LLC

All rights reserved. No part of this book may be reproduced or utilized in any form or by any means, electronic or mechanical including photocopying, recording, or by any information storage and retrieval system without permission in writing from the publisher.

www.rourkepublishing.com

PHOTO CREDITS: © Renee Brady: title page, page 4, 8; © Diane Rutt, © Diana Lundin, © Marcelo Wain: page 6, 7 ; © Matej Michelizza, © Georgy Markov, © Jim Jurica: page 10; © Marcelo Gabriel Domenichelli, © Sean MacLeay: page 14, 15; © Craig Veltri, © Tim McCaig: page 14, 15.

Editor: Robert Stengard-Olliges

Cover design by Nicola Stratford, bdpublishing.com

Library of Congress Cataloging-in-Publication Data

Harris, Nancy.
   Mashed potatoes : collecting and reporting data / Nancy Harris.
      p. cm. -- (Math focal points)
   Includes index.
   ISBN 978-1-60044-640-5 (Hardcover)
   ISBN 978-1-60044-684-9 (Softcover)
   1. Statistics--Graphic methods--Juvenile literature. I. Title.

   QA276.13.H37 2008
   001.4'33--dc22

                                        2007018016

Printed in the USA

CG/CG

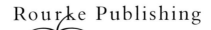

Rourke Publishing

www.rourkepublishing.com – rourke@rourkepublishing.com
Post Office Box 3328, Vero Beach, FL 32964

Table of Contents

Mashed Potatoes

Heather and Justin both love to eat mashed potatoes. They eat them for breakfast, lunch, and dinner. In fact, they even eat them for dessert!

Last week they made a chart to record which days they ate mashed potatoes.

Days We Ate Mashed Potatoes

Day	Heather	Justin
Sunday	Yes	Yes
Monday	No	Yes
Tuesday	Yes	Yes
Wednesday	Yes	Yes
Thursday	Yes	Yes
Friday	Yes	Yes
Saturday	No	Yes

Who ate mashed potatoes on Monday?
Which days did both kids eat mashed potatoes?

Breakfast

Today the kids recorded all the mashed potatoes they ate in one day. For breakfast, they ate hot mashed potatoes with toppings.

Their favorite breakfast toppings were:

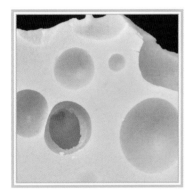
cheese

butter

scrambled eggs

Justin and Heather recorded what they ate on their breakfast mashed potatoes in a **picture graph**.

Toppings on Mashed Potatoes

	cheese		butter		scrambled eggs	
6	🧀					
5	🧀				🍳	🍳
4	🧀				🍳	🍳
3	🧀				🍳	🍳
2	🧀	🧀			🍳	🍳
1	🧀	🧀			🍳	🍳
	Heather	Justin	Heather	Justin	Heather	Justin

Which breakfast topping did they like best?
Which breakfast topping did they like least?

Heather ate three bowls of mashed potatoes and Justin ate two bowls of mashed potatoes for breakfast.

They made a **tally table**. It showed how many bowls of mashed potatoes they ate for breakfast.

Bowls for Breakfast

Kids	Tally	Number
Justin	II	2
Heather	III	3

How many bowls of mashed potatoes did they eat altogether? How many more bowls of mashed potatoes did Heather eat than Justin?

Lunch

At lunch the kids ate warm mashed potato pancakes with toppings.

Their favorite lunch toppings were:

applesauce

onions

sour cream

Heather made a **bar graph** to record how many toppings they put on their pancakes.

Toppings on Mashed Potato Pancakes

	applesauce		onions		sour cream	
6						
5						
4		▓				
3	▓	▓				
2	▓	▓			█	█
1	▓	▓			█	█
	Heather	Justin	Heather	Justin	Heather	Justin

How many toppings did the kids eat altogether?
Which topping did they eat the most of?

11

Justin made a tally table showing how many mashed potato pancakes they ate for lunch.

Number of Mashed Potato Pancakes

Kids	Tally	Number
Justin	IIII	4
Heather	II	2

*Who ate the most mashed potato pancakes?
How many fewer mashed potato pancakes did
Heather eat?*

Dinner

Dinner was hot mashed potatoes served with warm toppings.

Their favorite dinner toppings were:

meat

carrots

peas

Justin and Heather recorded what they ate on their dinner mashed potatoes in a picture graph.

Toppings on Mashed Potatoes

	meat		carrots		peas	
6	▪					
5	▪				▪	▪
4	▪				▪	▪
3	▪				▪	▪
2	▪	▪		🥕	▪	▪
1	▪	▪	🥕	🥕	▪	▪
	Heather	Justin	Heather	Justin	Heather	Justin

Which dinner toppings did the kids like the same? How much did they eat of these three toppings altogether?

Heather made a tally table. It showed how many plates of mashed potatoes they ate for dinner.

Plates of Mashed Potatoes Eaten

Kids	Tally	Number
Justin	I	1
Heather	II	2

How many plates of mashed potatoes did they eat altogether? How many fewer plates of mashed potatoes did Justin eat?

Dessert

Mashed potatoes for dessert was their favorite treat! They ate scoops of mashed sweet potatoes.

Their favorite dessert toppings were:

chocolate sauce

marshmallows

sprinkles

Heather put four teaspoons of chocolate sauce on top. Justin put five teaspoons of chocolate sauce on top.

Both put three teaspoons of marshmallows and one teaspoon of sprinkles on top.

The kids made a **table graph** to record what toppings they had on their dessert mashed potatoes.

Dessert Toppings Eaten

Toppings		Number
Chocolate sauce		9
Marshmallows		6
Sprinkles		2

How many servings of toppings did they eat in all? What was their favorite topping?

Justin and Heather made a tally table. It showed how many scoops of mashed sweet potatoes they ate for dessert.

Scoops of Mashed Sweet Potatoes Eaten

Kids	Tally	Number
Justin	I	1
Heather	IIII	4

How many total scoops of sweet mashed potatoes did the kids eat for dessert? Who ate the most dessert?

Too Many Mashed Potatoes

At the end of the day, Justin and Heather were stuffed. Look at the table graph. Did they eat too many servings of mashed potatoes today?

Mashed Potatoes Eaten During Each Meal

Meal	Servings
Breakfast	5
Lunch	6
Dinner	3
Dessert	5